Christian Evidence Series of i

EVIDENCE FOR THE RESURRECTION

by

John Austin Baker

Bishop of Salisbury

Published by Mowbray for
THE CHRISTIAN EVIDENCE SOCIETY

Copyright © John Austin Baker, 1986
ISBN 0 264 67113 9

First published 1986 for the Christian Evidence
Society by A.R. Mowbray & Co. Ltd., Saint Thomas
House, Becket Street, Oxford, OX1 1SJ.

Typeset by Getset (BTS) Ltd., Eynsham, Oxford
Printed in Great Britain by Tisbury Printing Works Ltd., Salisbury

Evidence for the Resurrection

The Evidence then and now

For those who heard the Easter story from the apostles and first followers of Jesus the 'evidence' must have had a very different force and status from any it can have now. These were eye-witnesses or friends or eye-witnesses. They could be cross-questioned, their character and credibility assessed. Some believed them, others did not; but either way it was the story itself which convinced or alienated.

Today, perhaps, few are brought to Christ primarily by the story itself. What persuades more often is a combination of the love and goodness of certain Christians, the personality and teaching of Jesus, and the Gospel message as a whole. But it is still very important, in a sceptical and often hostile culture, that the Easter story should stand up to attack – no easy matter at a distance of almost 2,000 years. But stand up it does.

What kind of evidence do we have?

In the eyes of some people it is silly even to talk of evidence. There is nothing to discuss. Resurrection from the dead is something that does not happen. To them one may at least suggest that it is unscientific not to consider whatever evidence there is. Then there are Christians who are happy to take the Easter stories as poetic expressions of spiritual truth, but feel that actual miracles of this sort are not the way God acts. The philosophical point is discussed by Professor Swinburne in the first booklet in this series, *Evidence for*

God. Here again, a look at the evidence may persuade them that God acts in more varied ways than they had supposed.

So what kind of evidence have we got? First, there is what may be called 'general' evidence, beginning with the fact of the Church. However badly the Church may fail to live up to its own ideals, however black some pages of its history may be, yet after two thousand years and with almost one billion members it must say something about the power of the beliefs on which it was founded. Perhaps indeed the very fact that it has experienced so many corruptions and failures but has always been renewed in goodness, love and fresh understanding of truth points more strongly than anything to an authentic reality at its heart.

Then, within the life of the Church we have the testimony of many Christians in every generation to their experience of Jesus as a living person. This is not just mystical experience. It leads to transformation of values and behaviour, of which the supreme example is perhaps that of the first disciples. From being frightended and broken people, with only a confused idea of his message, they became bold and joyful ambassadors, filled with his spirit, and ready to die for his cause. Moreover, Christians of every kind have been vividly aware in their lives of what we may call the 'Cross-and-Resurrection' pattern. It may be the gift of new strength when one's own resources are utterly spent; or the emergence of blessing and joy from what seemed total tragedy and disaster; miraculous healing of body or spirit, or ultimate victory for a good cause that seemed irretriveably lost. But whatever form it takes, it is constantly linked with prayerful trust in the Crucified and Risen Lord, and speaks to the believer of his continuing power and presence.

General observations of this kind may not carry much weight on their own, but they become much more significant when taken in conjunction with the particular evidence of the New Testament with which we shall from now on be concerned. For one thing they are, as already mentioned, the kind of consequences that ought to flow if the Resurrection claims are true. For another (and this is the reverse of the same coin) they underline that the particular evidence is concerned with far more than the bringing back to life of one isolated individual. The New Testament is not offering for our acceptance anything so cheap as a sensational marvel for its own sake. It asks us to see in the Easter event a revelation of the loving and universal purpose of God — and to this its results in the experience of the believer are highly relevant.

Turning then to the New Testament we find the Resurrection attested in almost every book. In the four Gospels there are, of course the stories of the first Easter. In Acts a great variety of material is presented. The letters of St Paul (except Philemon) not only refer constantly to the Resurrection but also contain discussions of its significance from many angles, and of our own resurrection in relation to it. Of the remaining books 1 Peter and Revelation give it most prominence. Some, such as Hebrews, Jude, and the three Letters of John, make little or no explicit reference to the actual Resurrection, but speak a good deal about closely related themes such as Christ's exaltation into heaven or the gift to us of eternal life through Christ. Only in James and 2 Peter might there be said to be no allusion at all, and even here there are certainly passages very hard to explain unless belief in Jesus's Resurrection is assumed (e.g., James 5.7, 14; 2 Peter 1.11).

But the central importance for the New Testament of the Resurrection is not shown simply in the constant occurrence of references to it, accounts of it, or thoughts about it. It is revealed also in something so frequent and fundamental that it is easily overlooked altogether. This is the application to Jesus by all writers, as a matter of course, of such titles as

'Lord', 'Christ' (i.e. 'Messiah') and 'Son of God'. These terms did not at that time have the full doctrinal meaning they were later given by the Church. Even so 'Lord' (*Kyrios*) was a title of God in the Greek version of the Old Testament, and an honorific of the divinized Roman Emperors. 'Messiah' was a term which no Jew could ever have applied to a man whose life had ended on a cross, since the Messiah was essentially a victorious Saviour hero. Similarly, 'Son of God' was a messianic title in the Old Testament, and for Christians inevitably brought with it reminders of Jesus's claim to a special relationship with God as his Father. How could that claim have stood after Good Friday, unless Jesus had been unmistakably vindicated by some sign of God's approval? But we do not need to rely on conjecture, however forceful. The New Testament states each point for us. In Acts, referring to the Resurrection, Peter is presented as saying on the day of Pentecost, 'Let all Israel then accept as certain that God has made this Jesus, whom you crucified, both Lord and Messiah' (Acts 2.36). St Paul, writing to the church in Rome, says: 'he was declared Son of God by a mighty act in that he rose from the dead' (Rom. 1.4). It is no exaggeration to say that wherever these titles of Jesus are found, faith in his Resurrection is the basis of them.

One other thing needs to be said at this stage if the evidence of the New Testament writings is to be properly assessed. That Jesus was crucified is regarded by any serious historian as a fact beyond dispute. To a Jew, however personally devoted to Jesus, this could at best be a tragic martyrdom, something to be reversed and erased when God finally came in judgement. But if one thing in the New Testament is more clear than any other it is that whatever happened at Easter was not seen as cancelling or correcting Good Friday. On the contrary, it glorified it, revealed it as part of God's purpose. The Good News preached in the New

Testament Church was not just the Resurrection but 'Cross-and-Resurrection', inseparably, as both integral parts of God's salvation. As we study the accounts of the disciples' Easter experiences, it will be important to remember that this was the indisputable outcome of those events, that it was not the outcome to be expected, and that the events themselves must therefore have contained its specific cause.

What kind of documents supply the evidence?

A question that has to be asked as we approach the New Testament evidence concerns the documents in which it is contained. Are they authentic? How near are they in time to the events of which they speak? We shall mainly be concerned with three sets of writings: the Letters of St Paul; the four Gospels; and the Acts of the Apostles.

Not counting Hebrews, now generally agreed not to be by Paul, there are thirteen Letters in all which are traditionally ascribed to him. On the authenticity of some of these there are varying degrees of doubt; but fortunately for us the ones most relevant to our subject are among the seven or eight most widely agreed to be genuine. As to date, all of them fall somewhere between the year AD 48-9 and 62, when Paul was martyred at Rome.

The Gospels are a more complex matter, and it is not easy to give a fair summary of scholarly opinion at the present time. Most experts would probably accept Mark and Luke as authors of the books that bear their names. Matthew is something of a mystery. That the fourth Gospel is connected in some way with the Apostle John would be common ground for many scholars, but argument continues vigorously on what exactly that connection is.

On the matter of dating, a majority would probably put Mark in the mid-60's. Matthew and Luke, each of whom made use of Mark's text, are therefore placed around

AD 80, with John later still. How few hard data there are on which to decide these questions, and how large a part therefore has inevitably to be played by scholarly 'hunch', can be seen, however, from the fact that the late Bishop John Robinson, author of *Honest to God*, and a much respected New Testament scholar, was able to make a good case for challenging all these accepted datings. In *Redating the New Testament* he argued that all the Gospels must come from before the destruction of the Jerusalem Temple by the Romans in AD 70; and much of the incidental evidence could fit as well into that time-scale. So far his views have not shifted the majority consensus, but the debate continues.

What, however, is widely (but quite wrongly) said, and needs to be corrected is this. The suggestion that the Gospels were written between thirty-five and sixty years after the Resurrection is taken to imply that anything they have to tell can have little historical value. But to argue is that way is to ignore most of what patient study in this century has been able to reconstruct of the way the Gospels probably came into being. They were not pure literary compositions, written up by an author after some personal research. The authors used materials, stories and sayings, which had already been formulated in the Christian community, and given some degree of fixed and memorable form for teaching and preaching purposes. They re-organised this, adapted it, built in their own theological comment; but its pre-history can still be partly discerned, especially in Mark, Matthew and Luke, which are so closely inter-related. John's treatment of his material is more complex, but that there are roots to it is still apparent. When we study the Easter stories in the Gospels, we are studying not just one writer's account but memory and proclamation reaching back eventually into the first Easter community itself.

Mention of 'proclamation' reminds us of another vital fact.

The Gospels are works of faith: they are written 'that you may hold the faith that Jesus is the Messiah, the Son of God, and that through this faith you may possess life by his name' (John 20.31). It has been said that the light of Easter falls backward over the whole Gospel story; and this is true. Indeed, had it not been for Easter, the Gospels would never have been written – not just because no one would have been interested in Jesus, but because, if someone is proclaimed as risen from the dead, people need to know more about him. Was this really the work of God? Was he truly a good man, a prophet, even the Messiah? What is God telling us by this unique miracle? To pursue this line of thought would take us far beyond our present brief. But it does remind us that from the start that the Church had a vital investment in history; and this extended to the Resurrection story itself. If there were no fact here, all was fraud. The foundations had to stand firm.

The Book of Acts is more quickly dealt with. It is the second volume of Luke's great history of the beginnings of Christianity, the sequel to his Gospel. As such its date will vary with the dating of that Gospel, but must fall somewhere between AD 65 and 90. Its importance for us lies immediately in its accounts of Paul's conversion, as a result of his meeting with the Risen Jesus on the Damascus road, and in its witness to the pattern of early Christian preaching of the Cross and Resurrection.

The primary witness: St Paul
By general agreement the foundation testimony to the Resurrection is that given by St Paul in his First Letter to the Corinthians, chapter 15, verses 1 – 11. Here Paul reminds his readers that he had passed on to them the authoritative summary of the Gospel which had been given to him, presumably not long after his conversion. We are, therefore,

in touch here with a basic, almost creed-like statement of faith, current most probably in the Jerusalem church some five years after the Resurrection.

It is extremely simple: 'Christ died for our sins, as the Scriptures had foretold; he was buried, he was raised on the third day, as the Scriptures had foretold; he appeared to Cephas, then to the Twelve.' The lapidary style, unadorned, uncommented, makes one thing quite clear. All four assertions are meant to be on the same level. That Christ was raised, and that he appeared, are as much facts, objective realities independent of observers, narrators or believers, as that he died and was buried. It should also be added that the word translated 'appeared' carried no overtones of 'apparition'. It is regularly used of flesh-and-blood people, as we might say, 'I was standing outside the bank when Mary appeared.'

It is likely that the original formula stopped with the reference to 'the Twelve', as above. The syntax changes at this point, and Paul himself probably added the mention of appearances to James, to all the apostles, and on one occasion to more than five hundred followers. The witness to these episodes is thus not so early as that of the opening statement. But, written probably in AD 52, it is still earlier than any other we have; and by linking these appearances to the one in his own life Paul shows the utmost seriousness and conviction as to their authentic reality.

The appearances of the Risen Christ

Any mighty spiritual event will stretch the powers of language to breaking-point and beyond. The experiences of those at the heart of it may well be impossible for them to convey adequately even to their friends, and harder still for those same friends to pass on to others. In the effort accepted religious precedents and images will be called upon to communicate what has been happening; and stories emerge which we call 'legends', intended perhaps to protect the truth from attack, or to express its meaning more in terms of 'how it must have been' than of any strong tradition of 'how it was'. Some of these stories, if not literally true are yet *ben trovato*, 'aptly invented'; others are less so. But alongside all these explanatory elaborations much of the original 'hard fact' also survives, carefully treasured. As we look now at the stories of Jesus's first followers concerning their experiences of his Resurrection presence among them, we shall see all these features, and have to try to judge which are which. You may not agree with my judgement, but that will not matter. There are no absolute certainties here. It is for each reader of the New Testament to make his or her own decisions in integrity.

The first point to note is that the New Testament offers no account at all of the actual Resurrection. (Later Christian writers felt the lack and made one or two attempts to fill it – very unconvincingly.) Not only was this wise, because such a miracle must be indescribable; but it also suggests a spirit of sober honesty which will speak only of what someone actually experienced.

We are, therefore, dealing primarily with 'appearance' stories; and to our astonishment the earliest Gospel, *Mark*, has none. Most scholars now seem to think that Mark's book ended with 16.8. Personally I disagree; but what is certain is that Mark's surviving writing ends there. If there ever was any more, it has been lost. So all that Mark himself can offer us is a visit, early on the Sunday morning, by three women followers, who find the Tomb open and empty, and a young man in a white robe. He tells them that Jesus is risen, and that they are to give the news to Peter and the other disciples, who are to go to Galilee and meet Jesus there. The story ends with the words, 'They fled from the tomb . . . and said

9

nothing to anyone, for they were afraid.'

'Who moved the stone?' Frank Morison took this question as his title for perhaps the most famous popular book on the Resurrection ever written. His own ingenious answer, like all others, has its difficulties. For Mark himself it was almost certainly just part of the Resurrection miracle, one factor in the numinous awe which fell upon the women. What is striking is that Mark, Luke and John all insist that the first arrivals at the cave-tomb did find the big circular door-stone rolled away. Only Matthew, as we shall see, alters the story, probably as part of his concern to counter the charge that Jesus's body had been stolen.

Matthew's story is far more complicated, but in basic essentials it follows Mark's lead fairly closely. Two women come to the tomb early, and are given the same message and instructions. That thread is, however, completed by a brief paragraph, saying that the disciples did go to Galilee, and did see Jesus, who commanded them to baptize and teach all nations, and assured them of his abiding presence with them.

The elaborations in Matthew are both religious and apologetic. An earthquake and an angel move the stone, and the angel gives the message. His appearance stuns a guard of soldiers put there to prevent Jesus's followers from stealing the body and then pretending that he had risen. But Matthew later alleges that this is in fact the story put about by Jewish enemies of the Church; and his account of the way the priests are supposed to have covered up the guards' failure lacks plausibility. Finally the women, on leaving the tomb, themselves meet the Risen Jesus who repeats the angel's message to the disciples.

It is *Luke* whose account is most radically different. For him there is no command to go to Galilee, nor any meeting with Jesus there. Everything happens in or near Jerusalem.

10

It is still the women who come early on Sunday to the tomb, and find it open and empty; but two angels who appear and tell them that Jesus is risen say nothing of a meeting in Galilee, but simply remind them that Jesus had himself predicted his Passion and Resurrection. The women then go to the apostles, and report what has happened, but are disbelieved.

It is now that Luke comes into his own. First there is the consummately beautiful story of the walk to Emmaus, when Jesus joins two disciples on the road, but is unrecognised. They tell him of the crucifixion and the news brought by the women, and he explains to them how all this had been foretold in Scripture. Heart-warmed by his words they persuade him to stay with them overnight; but when at supper he blesses and breaks the bread they recognise him and he vanishes. Returning at once to Jerusalem, they learn that Jesus has also appeared to Peter; and at that very moment he stands among them all. After further teaching, and a strict command to them to stay in Jerusalem until power for their future mission is given them from God, the day ends with Jesus leading them to Bethany, where he ascends to heaven.

Here for the first time we have significant details offered about the nature of the Resurrection appearances. On the one hand there is great stress on the reality of Jesus's body. He invites the disciples to handle him and to see for themselves that he has flesh and bones; he is no ghost. He even asks for food, and eats broiled fish, to prove the point. Yet he can vanish and appear at will, and is not always recognised.

John supplies the largest quantity of Resurrection material, but part is in what seems to be an appendix (chap. 21). His main story begins like the others with the visit to the Tomb, but presents this differently. Here only one woman comes – Mary Magdalene, the one common factor in all the versions. She finds the stone taken away, and assumes that

11

the body has been removed. Without checking, she runs and tells Peter and the beloved disciple, who come at once to the cave. They find the body gone, but the grave-clothes still there, the shroud in one place, the face-cloth used to tie up the jaw in another. They then 'return home'.

The story of Mary then resumes. She sees two angels, and then Jesus, whom she mistakes for the gardener, until he speaks her name. He gives her a message for his 'brothers' that he is ascending to God, which she delivers.

At evening Jesus appears to the disciples in the room in Jerusalem where they are gathered, and shows them his hands and side. He endows them 'holy spirit', and grants them authority to give or withhold forgiveness of sins. A week later he appears again, this time to reprove the disbelief of Thomas, who had been absent before, and to pronounce a blessing on all those future disciples who would believe without having seen him.

The second part of the story takes place in Galilee. Peter and six other disciples have been fishing all night without success. At dawn Jesus calls to them from the shore, but they do not recognise him. Only when he has guided them to a huge catch do they realise who it is. They disembark and breakfast as his guests. After breakfast Jesus puts to Peter three times the question, 'Do you love me?', confirms him in his leadership of the disciples, and foretells his martyrdom.

Finally, brief mention must be made of the testimony of *Acts*. A reference to Jesus eating and drinking with his disciples after the Resurrection links back to Luke's Gospel. But the major new element is the three accounts of Paul's meeting with the Risen Christ on the Damascus Road. Here the appearance is of dazzling light from which Jesus speaks to Paul. It is thus of a very different character from the Easter stories in the Gospels.

The common themes in the traditions

In all these narratives there are scores of illuminating details which there is no space to discuss. But by summarising the accounts in bald outline we can see more easily the themes and elements they share.

First, there is the insistence that one or more of *the women* followers of Jesus were first to discover the tomb, opened and empty, on Easter Day. There is no unanimity on all the names, but Mary Magdalene is agreed to have been one of them. This emphasis on the women is remarkable, because in Judaism at that time the testimony of women was not accepted to decide matters in a court of law. Why then give them this significant place, unless it were a remembered fact?

But was their place really significant? Was the Tomb empty? And does it matter? Today *the empty tomb* is often dismissed as most probably legend. But against this two points need to be underlined. First, the empty tomb, in the earliest traditions, is firmly linked with the visit by the women. Only John seems to feel a need to reinforce this with the evidence of two male disciples. Secondly, the empty tomb is not used as proof of the Resurrection. Matthew and John are both aware that the way the women found the stone already rolled back could mean that someone had taken the body, though only Matthew's tradition tries to counter this explanation. This lack of theological or defensive presentation strengthens the case for seeing the empty tomb as another element in the hard core of fact.

If this is accepted, we still have to ask what the significance of the Empty Tomb might be. Here the appearance stories and their strangely ambiguous witness to the nature of *the Resurrection body* have to be taken into account. Some features seem questionable. Did the risen Jesus really eat food? Luke is the only Gospel to state this explicitly. At the lakeside breakfast in John Jesus invites the disciples to eat, and distributes bread and fish to them, but is not said to eat himself. It is hard to think what the point of eating would be. Presumably resurrection life is eternal life, and a body capable of digesting food will not be eternal. Behind these stories may be many different influences, as, for example, the contemporary hope of an earthly messianic kingdom, or experiences of the Risen Lord during the breaking of bread in remembrance of him.

But even if these particular stories are legend, they also reflect a central theme of all the appearance stories. The Risen Jesus presents some strange features – he appears and vanishes within closed rooms, he is not always immediately recognised, he seems to be wearing clothes – but nevertheless the stories insist that he was not a 'ghost', a spirit manifestation, nor did he behave like one. This was a new mode of existence, a fullness of human life, and therefore not 'disembodied.'

It seems probable that it was this supra-physical quality, so far outside normal experience and so equally far beyond the reach of language, which led St Paul to elaborate his theory of the 'spiritual body', (1 Cor. 15.35 ff., cf. 2 Còr. 5.1-4). The corruptible physical body is like a seed. It is placed in the ground and disappears, but in its place is the wheat, something greater and more glorious. A similar miracle will transform those who are alive at the Last Day. Our bodies will be made like the Lord's glorious body (Phil. 3.21) – here Paul's own experience on the Damascus Road seems to be playing its part.

Within this framework the empty tomb fits very well. The divine miracle of resurrection is nothing to do with 'resuscitation'. The old body as such is no longer required, as ours will not be. But resurrection life is not a purely spiritual thing. Bodily existence is given a new, eternal form. Had the

14

tomb not been empty, this truth would have been much harder to grasp.

The risen body also perfectly expresses the inner reality of the person. (Hence perhaps the difficulties at first of recognising Jesus?) Thus the wounds in the hands, feet and side of the Risen Lord proclaim the Gospel of Cross-and-Resurrection combined. The marks of his death belong to the very heart of his being, self-giving love.

The last major question raised by the New Testament evidence is this: where did the Resurrection appearances take place? Though Luke's all-Jerusalem picture has shaped the traditional story, Galilee has the stronger claim. Mark, the earliest Evangelist, seems to envisage Galilee only. Matthew, even if he has little of his own to offer, knows of no reason to upset that emphasis – the appearance to the women is little more than a reinforcement of their message. The appendix to John gives us two Galilee appearance stories, and in a very significant context. The disciples have returned to their work as fishermen, something most unlikely if they had already had their mission charge, as in John 20. Psychologically the right place for these stories, including the reconciliation with Peter, is before the Resurrection encounters in Jerusalem, not after.

Yet one thing is certain. St Paul's contemporary testimony shows that the mother church of the Christian movement was in Jerusalem. It was from there that the good news went out. Luke's picture is true as church history. The likeliest conjecture (and it can be no more) is that after the first Easter Day, and the discovery of the empty tomb, the disciples returned to Galilee (which would have been safer anyway); that there they met the Risen Lord, and received their mission charge; and that they returned to Jerusalem, where in the power of the Spirit they proclaimed God's victory in the very place where his Christ had seemingly been defeated.

The beginning – and the End

One point remains to be made, and it is perhaps the strongest of all the evidences for the Resurrection. As everyone knows the earliest Church expected the end of this world-order and the coming of God's new dispensation, inaugurated by Jesus, in the near future. Why? Because Jesus had predicted it? That no doubt was part of the reason. But the decisive, convincing fact was surely the Resurrection itself. What does St Paul say? 'Christ was raised to life – the first fruits of the harvest of the dead' (1 Cor. 15.20). Resurrection was something looked for at the End, when God's Kingdom came. That Jesus had risen must mean that that End was near. That the Church's conviction of this was so strong testifies to the reality of the Resurrection events. And that remains true even though later generations of Christians have had to re-think the relation between the two, between the beginning of new life in Christ and the End of God's perfected purpose for his creation.